Spiders, Cl and Rocket Ships

ANTHOLOGY 1

Compiled by
Elspeth Graham and **Mal Pe**

OXFORD
UNIVERSITY PRESS

Contents

Stories with familiar settings

Flow *Pippa Goodhart* 6

Toots and the Upside Down House *Carol Hughes* 9

The Lie Spider *Pippa Goodhart* 13

Plays

Fantastic Mr Fox (novel) *Roald Dahl* 16

Fantastic Mr Fox (play) *adapted by Sally Reid* 17

Toad of Toad Hall *A. A. Milne* 21

Poems based on observation and the senses

Mary and Sarah *Richard Edwards* 24

I Asked the Little Boy Who Cannot See *Anon.* 26

Chips *Stanley Cook* 27

Spaghetti *Frank Flynn* 28

Shape poems

Spaghetti *Noel Petty* 30

Spider *Trevor Millum* 30

Information books

The Apollo 11 Spacecraft 31

Tree Frogs *Claire Llewellyn* 32

Roman Remains *Richard Wood* 34

Puppets *Helen and Peter McNiven* 36

Myths, legends, fables

The Pomegranate Seeds *Elspeth Graham* 38
Rip Van Winkle *retold by John Howe* 42
The Traveller and the Bear *retold by Vivian French* 44

Traditional stories

The Face in the Mirror *Maggie Pearson* 47
Beauty and the Beast *retold by Adèle Geras* 50
The Frog Prince *retold by Antonia Barber* 53
The Fwog Pwince *Kaye Umansky* 56
Turtle Prince? *Russell Hoban* 59

Performance poems

Phinniphin *Frank Collymore* 60
My Song *King D. Kuka* 62
Sampan *Tao Lang Pee* 63
Cows *James Reeves* 64
Ninety-Nine *Elizabeth Godley* 66

Instructions

An Amazing Astronaut 68
Hand Shadows *Atlanta Brown* 70
Me and My Pet Dog *TwoCan* 72
How to Cook Spaghetti 74
Create a Crater *Godfrey Hall* 75

Adventure and mystery stories

The Arctic Fox *Mary Ellis* 76
Vicky Fox *Berlie Doherty* 79
Beetle and the Biosphere *Susan Gates* 82
The Eagle has Landed *Andrew Donkin* 86

Stories by the same author

The Owl Tree *Jenny Nimmo* 88
The Stone Mouse *Jenny Nimmo* 90
The Red Secret *Jenny Nimmo* 93

Humorous poetry: poetry that plays with language

The Octopus *Ogden Nash* 95
Twickham Tweer *Jack Prelutsky* 96
It's Dark in Here *Shel Silverstein* 98
Eletelephony *Laura E. Richards* 99
Windy Nights *Rodney Bennett* 100
Weather *Eve Merriam* 101

Encyclopedia entries

Kingfisher Children's Encyclopedia 102
The Dorling Kindersley Science Encyclopedia 104

Letters

The Ladybird Question 106
The Ladybird Reply 107
Letters from Antarctica *Sara Wheeler* 108
A noticeboard 110

Thematic Links 112

Introduction

This is an *anthology* (it says so on the cover). What is an anthology? It's a collection. Perhaps a better word is *assortment*, like a chocolate assortment, one of those big boxes of chocolates that come in layers. Those chocolates are all different shapes and tastes; and the pieces in this anthology are like that. There are poems that are square and chunky, and there's one that's the shape of a spider. There's writing in the shape of a play and lots in the shape of a story.

Writing doesn't taste of anything, but it can describe feelings. In this assortment you'll find pieces that are funny, sad, thoughtful, strange, lonely, and happy. Like the insides of chocolates, colour is important, too. You'll meet the sad God of the Underworld looking at bright colours that hurt his eyes, and the cold silver of the moon, and a child who can only imagine those things. You'll also find three helpings of spaghetti, and some chips. You'll learn how to turn your hands into a snail and the very strange thing that a certain frog does with its eggs. You'll meet a stone that thinks it's a mouse – or is it a mouse that thinks it's a stone?

Like all assortments, you might find one that you don't like as much as the others. But that one might be your friend's favourite. So share this book, and enjoy it.

Mal Peet and Elspeth Graham

Flow

PIPPA GOODHART

The day had started hopefully.

'I want a dog,' Oliver told his parents at breakfast. 'I really want a dog.'

'I really want an elephant!' Sally butted in. Then things got silly as they often did between Sally and Dad.

'But you've already got an elephant!' Dad said, pulling Sally's ponytail.

'No, I haven't!'

'Yes, you have. Over there!' Dad said pointing to the old tin trunk by the window where Inkypuss lay in a smug hug of sleep.

'That's Inky, and she's a cat, you twit!' said Sally.

'Oh no, she isn't. I'll prove to you that she's an elephant, shall I?'

Great, thought Oliver. Dad was in a good mood. Perhaps he should ask again about a dog some time after school. Somehow when Oliver talked with Dad these days the fun wasn't there. Not as it was for Sally. With Oliver conversations got serious. But perhaps tonight…?

'Now to begin with, Sally, what colour are elephants?'

'Grey.'

'And what colour is Inkypuss?'

'She's mixed. Black and white mixed.'

'And what do you get if you mix black and white?'

'Grey, but…'

'Exactly!' said Dad. 'There you are then!'

Oliver's gaze wandered through the small panes of the kitchen window to the craggy sunlit fellside beyond. Only a week and a day until school broke up, and then the summer holidays. It would be brilliant if he could have a dog. He only half-listened to Dad and Sally.

'But elephants are big!'

'Ha, but just imagine that you are a mouse, Sally.'

'OK, I'm a mouse. So what?'

'So Inkypuss comes around the corner. Is she big, or is she small?'

'Big, but…'

'No buts. Told you so. She's an elephant!'

'But she hasn't got a trunk!'

'And what, Sally Clever Clogs Pilkington, is that thing that she is sleeping on at this very moment?'

'A trunk, but…'

'There you are then. Totally proven. We don't need an elephant because we've got one already. Now get ready for school, you two.'

I wonder how he'll argue against a dog? thought Oliver. I'll find out this evening.

There is more about dogs on pages 72 and 103.

Toots and the Upside Down House

Carol Hughes

BAM! Toots swung her foot against the leg of the chair. BAM! Her father had left her waiting (BAM!) stuck on a chair between two bookcases at a stinky old church fair (BAM!) while he went off and bought stinky old stamps. BAM! BAM! BAM!

Toots was sick of waiting. She pulled her bag onto her knee and glared across the crowded hall. There was no sign of her father, but Michael Lambert and Thomas Sweeney, two boys from school, were heading her way. Toots shrank back against the wall.

'Don't let them see me,' she whispered. 'Please don't let them…'

It was too late.

'Well, look who's here,' said a smarmy voice. Toots opened her eyes to find Thomas's freckled face only inches from her own. 'Hello, Toots. What have you got in your bag? Could it be a teddy bear?'

Toots hugged her bag to her chest.

'C'mon Toots, where's Fweddy Weddy today?' sniggered Michael, reaching for her bag. 'Is he in here?'

Toots punched his hand away.

'Leave me alone, or I'll call my father.'

'Oh yeah? And what's he going to do? Come running to protect you? He's on the other side of the hall. He's forgotten all about you.'

'No he hasn't, he'll be here in a minute.'

'Yeah?' Thomas was quick. He grabbed the bag and laughed as he tried to shake it out of her grasp. Toots held on tight.

'Get off,' she squealed.

The boys latched onto her bag and pulled together.

'Let go! Let go!' wailed Toots, kicking Thomas's shin.

'What's going on here?' demanded a woman with shiny orange hair. 'This isn't a bear garden! Go on, get out of it the lot of you!' The boys let go of the bag and fled into the crowd.

'Now what was all that about?' asked the woman angrily.

'They started it,' Toots replied. 'They were trying to get my teddy bear.'

The woman pursed her lips. 'Aren't you a little old to make such a fuss over a teddy bear? If I was your mother...'

'Hello, Toots,' interrupted Mr Small, the vicar. He touched the woman gently on the arm.

'Mrs Bacon? Might I have a word?' He smiled at Toots, then whispered something in Mrs Bacon's ear.

Toots stared at the floor. It wasn't hard to guess what the vicar was saying.

'If I look up now,' she thought, 'she'll be looking at me in that way. She'll smile one of those "poor little girl" smiles.' Toots hated those smiles; she'd seen so many. The lips always curved up like a normal smile, but the eyes remained all pinched and worried; the way people look at you when you're sick. ▪

The Lie Spider

PIPPA GOODHART

Izzy and her mum have woken up very early. They have been talking about what Mum would like for her birthday. Mum has decided that crocus bulbs would be just right. They'd be something lovely to look forward to in the spring.

'That's settled then. Come on, let's take a look outside and plan where my birthday bulbs will go.'

'Now? In the dark?'

'It's not really dark – look! The sun's on its way. Come on, Izz. Pull on a coat and let's watch our birthday dawn!'

Izzy took Dad's big gardening coat and slipped her feet into his huge wellington boots. Then she walked out into the chill, damp air of morning. The sky was pink and gold behind black silhouetted trees. Mum pointed.

'Look at that, Izz. Fairy diamonds!'

The lawn sparkled. It was covered in a delicate lacework of silver threads that bounced and quivered. All along the threads clung droplets of dew that glinted in the pink morning light.

'It's nothing to do with fairies,' said Izzy. She was giving up fairies along with lies and wishes and everything else like that. 'It's wet spider's webs.'

'I know, I know,' said Mum. 'It's gossamer. But isn't it magical? Isn't it more lovely than any gemstone you could ever buy?'

'It won't last.'

'Of course it won't. That's the beauty of it! It can't be taken and trapped in the claws of any ring. Nobody could ever take it and sell it.'

Mum stood behind Izzy and held her tight, her chin resting on the top of Izzy's head.

'This is a real birthday treat, Izz. To be here with you now and seeing this!'

'Do you believe in magic, Mum?'

'On mornings like this I do!'

'If you could have anything you wanted, what would you ask for?'

Mum thought for a moment. 'I'm very happy with what I've got really. Perhaps a bit more time and...'

'...Peace!' laughed Izzy. 'I know!'

15

Fantastic Mr Fox

Roald Dahl

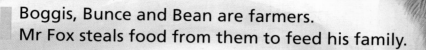

> Boggis, Bunce and Bean are farmers.
> Mr Fox steals food from them to feed his family.

'Dang and blast that lousy beast!' cried Boggis.

'I'd like to rip his guts out!' said Bunce.

'He must be killed!' cried Bean.

'But how?' said Boggis. 'How on earth can we catch the blighter?'

Bean picked his nose delicately with a long finger. 'I have a plan,' he said.

'You've never had a decent plan yet,' said Bunce.

'Shut up and listen,' said Bean. 'Tomorrow night we will all hide outside the hole where the fox lives. We will wait there until he comes out. Then… *Bang! Bang-bang-bang.*'

'Very clever,' said Bunce. 'But first we shall have to find the hole.'

'My dear Bunce, I've already found it,' said the crafty Bean. 'It's up in the wood on the hill. It's under a huge tree…'

There is more about foxes on pages 17, 76, 79 and 93.

Fantastic Mr Fox

ADAPTED BY SALLY REID

BOGGIS [*Banging fists on table*]: Dang and blast that lousy beast!

BUNCE: I'd like to rip his guts out!

BEAN [*Sinister*]: He must be killed.

BOGGIS: Hundreds of chickens have I lost to that sly fox. Night after night I've gone out after him with my gun, and night after night has he given me the slip. But I'll get him, and when I do he'll be in that pot, stewing along with the dumplings. Fox stew, that's what I'll be having. Ha ha!

BUNCE: Not if I get my hands on him first he won't. I'll be cooking his liver and mashing it up to put in my doughnuts. He'll not be eating many more of my ducks, I'll be telling you. I'll catch him one day – you mark my words, I've got to catch him.

BEAN [*Coolly*]: All I want to see is his rotten carcass hanging up in my cellar. Strung up [*Savouring the picture*] so he can never sneak in and take one of my plump turkeys ever again. He's outwitted us for too long now. He's made absolute fools of us. Every time we get near him, he heads off in the other direction. It's almost as if he smells us on the wind.

BUNCE: Us? How could he smell us? I wash every Friday.

BEAN [*Moving to front of tables, centre stage*]: He must be killed.

BOGGIS [*Moving beside* **BEAN**]: But how? How on earth can we catch the blighter?

[**BUNCE** *moves to join them*]

BEAN: I have a plan...

BUNCE: You've never had a decent plan yet.

BEAN: Shut up and listen. Things are a little different now. I have been thinking – an activity unknown to either of you. Tomorrow night we will all hide just outside the hole where the fox lives. We will be silent. We will be patient. And what is more, we will choose our positions *very* carefully. We will make sure that the wind is not blowing from us towards the fox's hole. That way we shall not be 'smelled out'. We will wait there until he comes out then...BANG, BANG, BANG!

BUNCE: Very clever, *very* intelligent. Just one thing, first we have to find the hole.

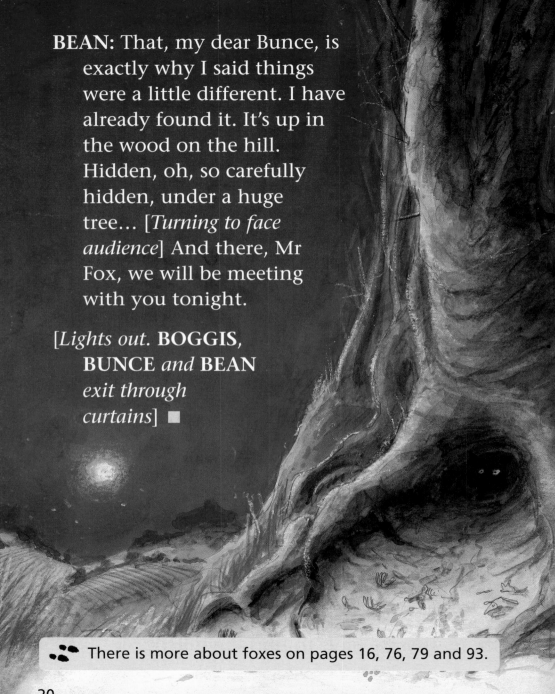

BEAN: That, my dear Bunce, is exactly why I said things were a little different. I have already found it. It's up in the wood on the hill. Hidden, oh, so carefully hidden, under a huge tree… [*Turning to face audience*] And there, Mr Fox, we will be meeting with you tonight.

[*Lights out.* **BOGGIS**, **BUNCE** *and* **BEAN** *exit through curtains*] ■

There is more about foxes on pages 16, 76, 79 and 93.

Toad of Toad Hall

A. A. MILNE

Mr Toad is in big trouble. He was arrested for wild driving in a stolen car, and then he was very cheeky to the police. Now, he is in court. Toad's enemy, the Chief Weasel, has managed to sneak onto the jury, disguised as a rabbit.

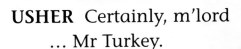

USHER Certainly, m'lord … Mr Turkey.

TURKEY Here!

USHER Mr Duck.

DUCK Here!

USHER Four squirrels!

SQUIRRELS Here!

USHER Six rabbits!

RABBITS Here!   **RAT** *rises and holds up his hand.*

RAT (*firmly*) I object.   *Sensation.*

JUDGE (*putting on his glasses*) What's the matter? Who is it? What did he— Ah, Ratty, my little friend, is it you? Delighted to see you. If you will just wait until I have got this ruffian off my hands, we can have a little talk. What about lunching with me? (*To* **USHER**) Go on, please.

USHER Six rabbits!

RABBITS Here!

RAT I object, my lord.

JUDGE (*surprised*) Object?

RAT One of the rabbits is a weasel.

CHIEF WEASEL (*indignantly*) I'm not! I'm a rabbit.

RAT He's a weasel.

JUDGE Dear, dear! A different of opinion. (*To* **USHER**) What are we to do? What *does* one do?

USHER He *says* he's a rabbit, my lord, and he ought to know.

JUDGE (*to* **RAT**) There's something in that. You can't make a mistake about a thing of that sort.

RAT (*doggedly*) He's a weasel.

CHIEF WEASEL I'm not.

RAT That proves it. (*To* **WEASEL**) Why should you say you aren't, if you aren't?

JUDGE But of course he says he aren't if he aren't.

I mean *if* he aren't, then he aren't, so naturally he says he aren't. *He fans himself with his handkerchief.*

RAT But he wouldn't *say* he wasn't, if he wasn't. The other rabbits didn't say they wasn't. Why didn't they say they wasn't. Because they aren't.

JUDGE (*to* **USHER**) Just make a note that I shall want a glass of iced water if this goes on.

RAT (*eagerly*) Of course if you aren't, you don't say you aren't, but if you weren't, you would say you were.

JUDGE (*completely muddled*) But you wouldn't say you aren't, if you weren't, and on the other hand— (*Despairingly*) I think we'd better begin this trial *all* over again.

USHER Yes, my lord. Much the best way.

JUDGE (*to* **RAT**) You can tell me your objections afterwards, when we have this desperate ruffian safely locked in a dungeon.

RAT He's a weasel! I know he's a weasel! You can see he's a weasel! It isn't fair!

Mary and Sarah

RICHARD EDWARDS

Mary likes smooth things,
Things that glide:
Sleek skis swishing down a mountainside.

Sarah likes rough things,
Things that snatch:
Boats with barnacled bottoms, thatch.

Mary likes smooth things,
Things all mellow:
Milk, silk, runny honey, tunes on a cello.

Sarah likes rough things,
Things all troubly:
Crags, snags, bristles, thistles, fields left stubbly.

Mary says — polish,
Sarah says — rust,
Mary says — mayonnaise,
Sarah says — crust.

Sarah says — hedgehogs,
Mary says — seals,
Sarah says — sticklebacks,
Mary says — eels.

Give me, says Mary,
The slide of a stream,
The touch of a petal,
A bowl of ice-cream.

Give me, says Sarah,
The gales of a coast,
The husk of a chestnut,
A plate of burnt toast…

Mary and Sarah—
They'll never agree
Till peaches and coconuts
Grow on one tree.

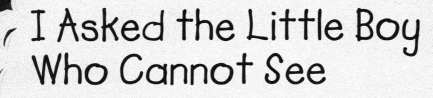

I Asked the Little Boy Who Cannot See

ANON.

I asked the little boy who cannot see,
'And what is colour like?'
'Why, green,' said he,
'Is like the rustle when the wind blows through
The forest; running water, that is blue;
And red is like a trumpet sound; and pink
Is like the smell of roses; and I think
That purple must be like a thunderstorm;
And yellow is like something soft and warm;
And white is a pleasant stillness when you lie
And dream.'

There is more about colour on page 38.

Chips

STANLEY COOK

Out of the paper bag
Comes the hot breath of the chips
And I shall blow on them
To stop them burning my lips.

Before I leave the counter
The woman shakes
Raindrops of vinegar on them
And salty snowflakes.

Outside the frosty pavements
Are slippery as a slide
But the chips and I
Are warm inside.

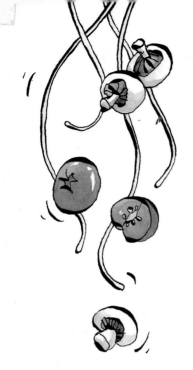

Spaghetti

FRANK FLYNN

A plate heaped high
with spaghetti
all covered with tomato sauce
is just about my favourite meal.
It looks just like
a gigantic heap of:
steaming
        tangled
     mixed
         up
twizzled
       twisted
wound
   up
     woozled
WORMS!

I like picking them up
one at a time;
swallowing them slowly
head first,
until the tail flips
across my cheek
before finally wriggling
down my throat.
But best of all,
when I've finished eating
I go and look in a mirror
because the tomato sauce
smeared around my mouth
makes me look like a clown.

There is more about spaghetti on pages 30 and 74.

Spaghetti

NOEL PETTY

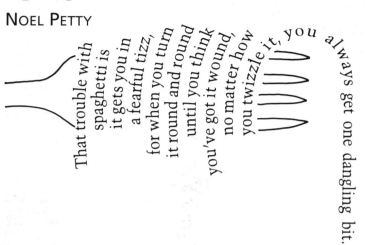

That trouble with spaghetti is it gets you in a fearful tizz, for when you turn it round and round until you think you've got it wound, no matter how you twizzle it, you always get one dangling bit.

One day I'll follow all the bends until I've found a pair of ends.

There is more about spaghetti on pages 28 and 74.

Spider

TREVOR MILLUM

a thousand eggs
trapping flies
Spying eyes
SPIDER
Spindle legs
SPIDER!

30

The Apollo 11 Spacecraft

On 21st July 1969, American astronauts became the first humans to walk on the moon. They had travelled there in a spacecraft called *Apollo 11*. *Apollo* had been lifted out of Earth's atmosphere by the huge, three-stage *Saturn 5* rocket – the biggest that had ever been built. The three astronauts returned safely to Earth in the Command module *Columbia* on 24th July.

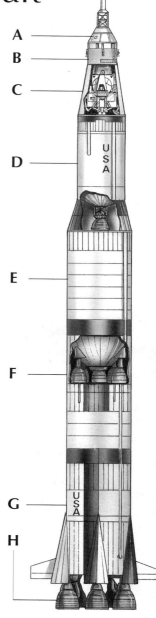

Apollo Flight Timetable	KEY
July 16: Lift-off from Cape Canaveral, Florida	**A** Command module (*Columbia*)
	B Service module
July 20: Eagle lunar module lands on moon	**C** Lunar module (*Eagle*)
July 21: Astronauts Armstrong & Aldrin walk on moon	**D** Third stage
	E Second stage
	F Engines
July 24: Columbia lands in Pacific Ocean	**G** First stage
	H Five engines

Tree Frogs

CLAIRE LLEWELLYN

1 Not all frogs live on the ground – Tree frogs spend almost all their lives up in trees. There are lots of different kinds, and this bright-green one is called a *Phyllomedusa.*

2 It lives among shiny green leaves in the South American rainforest, and its skin colour helps it to hide from birds and other enemies.

3 Most frogs lay their eggs in water, but not this Tree frog. The female looks for a branch overhanging a pond, and lays her eggs on a leaf.

4 She climbs down the tree afterwards, to sit in the pond and let the water soak in through her skin. Then she climbs back up to her eggs – and wees all over them! This makes the eggs swell up, and keeps them damp and jelly-like.

5 In just a few days, the eggs are ready to hatch. The tiny tadpoles drop down into the pond, where they live and grow until they change into frogs – and return to the trees.

There is more about frogs on pages 53, 56 and 59.

Roman Remains

RICHARD WOOD

A Sticky Situation

Have you ever sat on the loo, then realized, too late, that the paper has run out? The Romans never had this problem. Instead of paper, they used a piece of natural sponge fixed on a short wooden handle. In front of the loo was a water channel where people dipped their sponge-sticks. The same sponges were shared by everyone who used the loo.

Soldiers using the latrines at Housesteads, a fort on Hadrian's Wall in Northumberland. Notice the sponges and washing facilities.

A Stream of Gold

The Emperor Vespasian made money from public urinals that he built in the amphitheatre called the Colosseum. People had to pay to use them. Their urine was then collected and sold to cloth-makers, who used it to remove grease from wool.

A Soft Touch

Before going about his business, a Roman soldier would first select his sponge-stick. He would then clean this in the salty water or vinegar that was provided. Most Roman loos were designed with the sponge-stick in mind. The keyhole-shaped hole in the loo allowed the user to poke the sponge in and wipe himself. Rich Roman ladies did not like to use the sponge. They preferred the soft touch of an ostrich feather.

Puppets

HELEN AND PETER MCNIVEN

The first puppets were made a very long time ago. Ancient peoples used puppets to act out stories and to please their gods. Each puppet would be specially made for the part it would play.

Rod puppet

You can sometimes see puppets at festivals and at the seaside.

Today, puppet theatres still travel around the world telling stories which are very many years old.

There are four main types of puppet:

A glove puppet is worn on your hand, just as you would wear a glove. When you move your hand and fingers, the puppet moves.

A rod puppet has sticks fixed to the hands and head. You move the sticks to move the puppet.

Shadow puppets are simple flat shapes, sometimes brightly coloured. If you hold them up behind an old sheet and shine a light from behind the puppets, you will see their shadows on the sheet.

Shadow puppets

A string puppet is also called a marionette. It hangs on strings which you move to make the puppet do things like walk or dance.

You can make puppets out of almost anything. Most puppets can be made with things you will find easily at home and at school.

String puppets

The Pomegranate Seeds

Elspeth Graham

Hades is the God of the Underworld, where everything is dim and colourless. One day, he decides to visit the Overworld to remind himself what colour is like.

Hades travelled through secret twisting tunnels and caves, up and up and up. At last, he came to a cave filled with beams of sunlight. He screwed up his painful eyes and peered out at the Overworld. The colours! He was looking at a warm spring morning. He was looking at a meadow speckled with wild flowers, white and yellow and pink. Further away, light sparkled on blue sea. Further away still, pale purple mountains rose towards a clear blue sky. He remembered the word *green*. Yes, that was it. Green. There were so many different kinds of green. The different greens of grass, of plants, of trees, of the shadows of trees and plants on the grass. Hundreds of shades of green! Amazing! Hades grew dizzy looking at them. The pain in his eyes spread into his head. He had to go back, back down to the dim grey world that did not hurt his eyes. Then Hades heard a voice, the voice of someone alive, someone singing. He turned to see where it was coming from. Then he fell in love, just like that.

He fell in love with a girl called Persephone. Persephone had skin the colour of honey and hair like black silk. She was walking across the meadow, picking flowers. Her dress was the same blue as the blue of the sky, and she was singing. She was beautiful.

Hades didn't stop to think. He just stepped out into the painful sunlight and grabbed Persephone. He grabbed her and carried her back down the secret twisting tunnels, down towards his Underworld.

Now, this is a story about gods and goddesses.

There aren't any ordinary human people in this story. Persephone was the daughter of gods. Her father was Zeus, the greatest of the gods. Her mother was Demeter, the goddess of nature, of all that grows on Earth. Demeter made seeds turn into plants. She made buds grow into flowers.

She made fruit grow on trees and plants. She was a kind and gentle goddess. She spread warmth through the world.

But when Demeter found that her daughter Persephone had disappeared she was filled with anger and sadness.

There is more about colour on page 26.

Rip Van Winkle

RETOLD BY JOHN HOWE

> Rip has been walking in the mountains and has met a strange little man carrying a barrel. Rip offers to carry the barrel.

As they went along Rip every now and then heard long rolling peals, like distant thunder, that seemed to come from a deep ravine between the rocks above them. He paused for a moment, but supposing the sound to be the muttering of one of those thunderstorms that often take place in the mountains, he went on.

They finally came to a small circular hollow, and when they entered, Rip saw a company of small men playing at long pins. What a strange group they were! One had a large beard and small piggish eyes. The face of another seemed to consist entirely of nose, and he wore a tall gray hat set off with a pink feather. They all had beards of various shapes and colours, and the longest one belonged to the one who seemed to be the commander. He was a stout old gentleman with a weather-beaten face.

Rip greeted them politely, but they answered not a word. Nothing, indeed, interrupted the stillness of the scene but the noises of the balls. When they were rolled, they echoed along the mountains like rumbling peals of thunder.

Rip and his companion came closer. The men suddenly stopped their play and stared at him in a way that made his heart flip within him and his knees knock together.

The Traveller and the Bear

Retold by Vivian French

"Twinkle twinkle, little stars!"
Sang the man as he walked with the bear.
"Twinkle twinkle, little stars!
Can you see the stars in the velvet sky?
See them watching us, you and I!"

The bear said nothing.
The bear padded on, watching the rough and
    stony ground beneath his feet.
The trees whispered and murmured in the night
And dark shadows lay across the way.
The bear padded on, and on, and on.

"Hey there, bear! Look up and see
See how the stars wink down at me!
Why do you stare at the dank dark ground?
The heavens are glittering all around..."

And still the bear looked down...
And still the bear padded on, and on, and on...

"Look up! Look up to the sparkling sky
Or the stars will laugh as you pass them by –"

CRASH!!!!!!!!!!!!!!
                    SPLASH!!!!!!!!!!!!!!

Roly poly roly poly roly poly into the ditch.

The bear looked up and he shook his head.
"There's a time", he said, "for looking at stars
And a time to look at the road ahead."

The man muttered
And sputtered his way out of the ditch.
"If ever the stars were laughing
They're laughing now," he said.

The Face in the Mirror

MAGGIE PEARSON

Look in any mirror, and what do you see?
Your own face, of course. You know it is.
But what would you think if you had never
seen a mirror before?

Long, long ago, there lived a man who owned
the only mirror in the world. How he came by it
I don't know, but from that day on, he was
never happy again, for that mirror told lies.

It kept telling him he was getting older. He knew that this wasn't so. He could see his friends growing older, but he was still the same young man that he had always been. Wasn't he?

Yet every time he looked in the mirror, it showed another grey hair, another wrinkle.

The man shut the mirror away in an old tin chest, and never looked at it again.

But, of course, he still continued to grow older, as people do. And as old men do, at last he died.

Some days later his son was sorting through his father's things and came across the old tin chest. He opened it and looked inside.

What did he see?

He saw the mirror, but as no one had ever seen one before, he exclaimed:

"Why, it's a picture of

my father as a young man! How surprised he looks, to be having his picture painted!"

He sighed, and looked sad. "I do miss him so."

Wonder of wonders! The face gazing back at him was suddenly sad, too.

"Why, that almost looks like a tear running down my father's cheek," said the son.

Beauty and the Beast

RETOLD BY ADÈLE GERAS

> To save his own life, a merchant has promised to give one of his daughters to the Beast. He brings Belle, his youngest daughter, to the Beast's house. The house is grand and comfortable, and Belle says that living here could not be too terrible.

"You have not seen the Beast," said the merchant shivering. "Oh, you will change your tune when you do, my dear."

The door opened at their touch, just as it had before.

"We have come," the merchant called out, "as I promised."

His words floated up towards the ceiling, but no-one appeared.

"Come," said the merchant. "Let us go into the

banqueting hall and eat, for we have had a long journey, and you must be hungry, my dear."

Two places had been set at the table. Belle and her father were eating with heavy hearts when the Beast came silently into the room. It was only when he spoke that Belle caught sight of him, hidden in the shadows by the door.

"Is this the daughter," said the Beast, "who comes here in your place?"

"Yes, I am," Belle answered for her father. "My name is Belle and I am happy to be in such a beautiful house, and happy to be of service to my father."

"You will not be so happy," said the Beast, "once you have looked upon my face. It will fill you with horror and haunt all your dreams."

For her father's sake, Belle knew she had to be brave. She said, "I have heard your voice, sir, and it is as low and sweet a voice as any man ever spoke with. Your face holds no terrors for me."

The Beast stepped out of the shadows by the door, and the light of all the lamps in the room fell on his face. Belle's hands flew to cover her eyes, to shield them from the hideous sight, and it was with great difficulty that at last she peeped between her fingers at the Beast.

"Now," he said, "are you as ready as you were a moment ago to spend your days with me?"

Belle was quiet for a full minute, then she said, "I will become used to looking at you, sir, and then I will not flinch as I did just now. You must forgive me for my cruelty. It was the unexpectedness of seeing you for the first time. I shall not hide my eyes again."

The Frog Prince

RETOLD BY ANTONIA BARBER

> A beautiful princess loses her golden ball in a pond.
> A frog – who can talk – offers to rescue it. All he wants
> as a reward is to eat at the princess's table and sleep on
> her pillow. She doesn't like the idea much, but agrees.

So the princess lifted him up and then, tired out after her tantrums, she put her head down on her pillow and closed her eyes. And the little frog sat on the corner of her pillow and told her a long story which was exciting, and sad, and funny, and all the things a good story should be. As he told the story he drew closer and closer until, at the end, he sat beside her sleepy head.

The princess gave a contented sigh. "That was the best story ever, frog," she said. Through drooping eyelids she saw his friendly face and goggle eyes close to her own and found to her surprise that she rather liked them. "Goodnight, frog," she said, and she gave him a small peck of a kiss on the side of his funny green head.

What happened next had her leaping out of bed in astonishment. There was a blinding flash of light, a huge puff of smoke and a noise like a clap of thunder. And there, where the little green frog had been, was the most handsome prince the king's daughter had ever seen.

His eyes were kind and beautiful, if a little dazed, and he seemed rather embarrassed to find himself sitting on the princess's pillow.

The noise brought the king, the courtiers and all the princess's sisters running upstairs, and the prince explained to them all how he had been bewitched many years before by a particularly nasty witch. He had fallen foul of her when only a boy and had spent many weary years seeking a princess who would kiss him and break the spell.

Everyone was amazed at his story except the wise king, who had rather suspected something of the sort. "After all," he told them, "it's not every day you meet a frog who can talk."

Of course the prince and the princess fell deeply in love with each other. In due time they were married and lived together happily ever after. And if the youngest princess sometimes called her beloved husband "Frogface", she only did it when they were alone together.

 There is more about frogs on pages 32, 56 and 59.

The Fwog Pwince

Chapter 1
In Which We Meet Prince Pipsqueak

'Once upon a time, there was a handsome young Prince who had the misfortune to offend a wicked Witch. In order to avenge herself, the Witch cast a spell over the Prince, turning him into an ugly frog.'

Well now. Let's get the facts straight. Prince Pipsqueak certainly wasn't handsome. Oh, he was a Prince all right. You could tell that at a glance. At least, you could before he got turned into a frog. After that, of course, it was a bit more difficult.

Here's Prince Pipsqueak before.

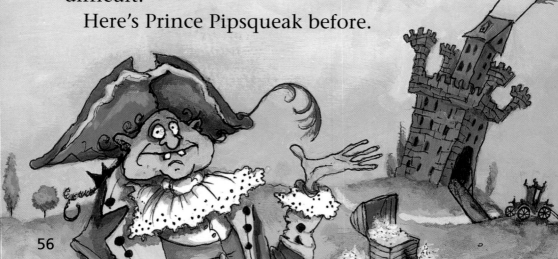

And here he is after.

You have to admit that the Witch did a thorough job.

Take a good look at the 'before' Pipsqueak. Note the princely trappings. Castle with attached moat. Crown, horse, coach, servants, smart clothes, room of his own, far too much pocket money and ridiculously expensive shoes.

Of course, if you took all that away, he would seem perfectly ordinary. Until he opened his mouth, that is. When he did that, he used A Certain Tone Of Voice – and you could tell right away that he wasn't normal.

Oooh. That Tone Of Voice. It was bold, brash

and bossy. It was snooty, snobby and sneery. It was haughty, high-handed and hoity-toity. It cut through conversations like a hedge-trimmer cuts through privet.

'I say! Peasant. Thwow down your cloak. I the Pwince wish to cwoss over this puddle!'

'You there! Waiter. This cup is cwacked. Don't you know I'm the Pwince?'

'Take me to the palace, cabby, and look sharp about it! What d'you mean *pay* you? I'm the Pwince!'

'I don't believe it! I simply don't *believe* it!! I'm the Pwince, and nobody's fluffed up my *thwone* cushion again!'

See what I mean? Let's face it. Prince Pipsqueak had a way of saying things that was guaranteed to get people's backs up. It got waiters' backs up. It got cab drivers' backs up. It got the servants' backs up. It even got his mother's back up (his mother, of course, being the Queen. Queen Mona).

There is more about frogs on pages 32, 53 and 59.

Turtle Prince?

RUSSELL HOBAN

Jim Frog sat on a lily pad;
he was feeling lonesome, feeling sad,
feeling more than somewhat fed-up
when a snapping-turtle stuck her head up
(caused a few ripples round the pond),
said, "Hello, sailor! Do not despond!
I fancy you, and I'll be quite frank –
although I'm of superior rank
(I'm a turtle princess actually),
I'm asking you to marry me.
This offer is too good to miss;
now, how about a great big kiss?"

Jim knew the stories; he'd read the books.
He didn't really like her looks;
her forthright manner made him wince,
but still, he thought – a turtle prince!
So he kissed her. I haven't seen him since.

 There is more about frogs on pages 32, 53 and 56.

Phinniphin

(CARIBBEAN)
FRANK COLLYMORE

The tide is in,
    The tide is in,
        The Phinniphin
            Are out.

They love the sea,
    The salty sea,
        Of this there is
            No doubt.

O watch them flop
    And slip and slop
        With clumsy hop
            Right past

The sandy beach
   Until they reach
      The friendly sea
      At last.

But when the tide,
   The shifty tide
      Stays right outside
      The bar,

They can't go in
   The Phinniphin;
   The Phinniphin
      Cannot go in:
         They'd have to hop
         Too far.

My Song

AMERICAN INDIAN (BLACKFOOT)
KING D. KUKA

Sitting, legs crossed, copper-toned old man
Chanting in low bass.
    'Ho aa Hey yah'
    'Way ah Hey ah'
Black Wolf is singing to the morning.
    'Hey aa ah Hey'
    'Way ah Hey aa'
He is singing to many years ago.
    'Hey ah Way Hey'
    'Way ah Hey aa'
The singing stops.
Drum silent.
Black Wolf looks down at his drum.
He has sung.

Sampan

(CHINESE)
TAO LANG PEE

Waves lap lap
Fish fins clap clap
Brown sails flap flap
Chop-sticks tap tap
Up and down the long green river
Ohe Ohe lanterns quiver
Willow branches brush the river
Ohe Ohe lanterns quiver
Waves lap lap
Fish fins clap clap
Brown sails flap flap
Chop-sticks tap tap

Cows

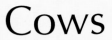

(British)
James Reeves

Half the time they munched the grass,
    and all the time they lay
Down in the water-meadows, the lazy
    month of May,
  A-chewing,
  A-mooing,
To pass the hours away.

'Nice weather,' said the brown cow.
  'Ah,' said the white.
'Grass is very tasty.'
  'Grass is all right.'

Half the time they munched the grass,
    and all the time they lay
Down in the water-meadows, the lazy
    month of May,
  A-chewing,
  A-mooing,
To pass the hours away.

'Rain coming,' said the brown cow.
    'Ah,' said the white.
'Flies is very tiresome.'
    'Flies bite.'

Half the time they munched the grass,
        and all the time they lay
Down in the water-meadows, the lazy
        month of May,
    A-chewing,
    A-mooing,
To pass the hours away.

'Time to go,' said the brown cow.
    'Ah,' said the white.
'Nice chat.' 'Very pleasant.'
    'Night.' 'Night.'

Half the time they munched the grass,
        and all the time they lay
Down in the water-meadows, the lazy
        month of May,
    A-chewing,
    A-mooing,
To pass the hours away.

Ninety-Nine

ELIZABETH GODLEY

THE DOCTOR. Good morning, and How do you do?
Pray what is the matter with you?

THE PATIENT. I've a cough and a sneeze
And two very bad knees
And a toe that is bothering, too.

THE DOCTOR. Hum, hum. I'll run over your chest—
Will you kindly unbutton your vest?
Now say 'Ninety-nine.'
Can you sleep? Can you dine?
You say you're not feeling your best?

THE PATIENT. I'm feeling exceedingly ill.

THE DOCTOR. Hum, hum. Can you swallow a pill?

THE PATIENT. No, no.

THE DOCTOR. Speak up louder!

THE PATIENT. NO, NO!

THE DOCTOR. A grey powder…
Let's see…In some jam.

66

THE PATIENT *(who likes jam)*.   As you will.

THE DOCTOR.   Ha, ha. Tra-la-la! Tootle-oo.
Now I'll tell you a thing that is true:
You can say '*Ninety-nine*',
You can sleep, you can dine—
There's nothing the matter with you!

THE PATIENT *(in a loud voice)*.
Nothing the matter with me?
How can that possibly be?
I've a sneeze and a cough,
And a toe nearly off,
And a horrible—

THE DOCTOR.   Fiddle-de-dee!

(They glare at one another.)

THE DOCTOR.   And now there is business to do.

(Pause.)

THE PATIENT *(in a very feeble voice)*.
I have only a penny or two…
If you speak of your fees—

THE DOCTOR.   Fifty pounds, if, you please!
There's nothing the matter with you.

An Amazing Astronaut

The astronaut on the opposite page is all dressed up and ready for his walk on the moon. Decorate his space suit with all sorts of shiny bits and pieces. Then make a border of his footprints around the edge of the picture (see paint tip).

Bits and Pieces
- Yellow, pink and red card
- Scissors and glue
- Corrugated card
- Paints and brush
- Silver foil
- Foil pie tin
- Cling film
- Drinking straws
- Paper shapes
- Polystyrene and foil shapes

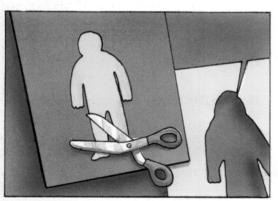

1 Cut the astronaut suit out of stiff yellow paper. Stick it on to the red card, as shown.

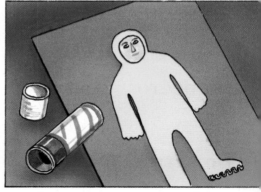

2 Glue on corrugated card boot soles, silver foil gloves and a painted card face.

3 Cut out the bottom of a foil pie tin. Cover the hole with cling film. Glue the tin over the face.

4 Glue badges, straws, paper, polystyrene and foil decorations on the space suit.

Paint tip

Cut a footprint from corrugated card. Brush watery paint all over the bumpy bits of the card. Then press it firmly on to the red card. Paint all the footprints going in the same direction.

 There is more about the moon and space travel on pages 31, 75, 86 and 104.

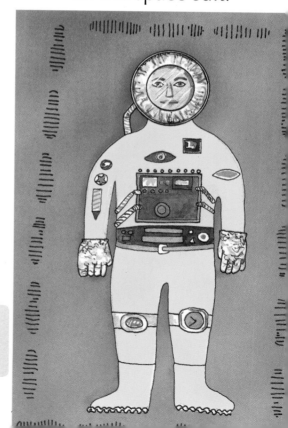

Hand Shadows

ATLANTA BROWN

Crab

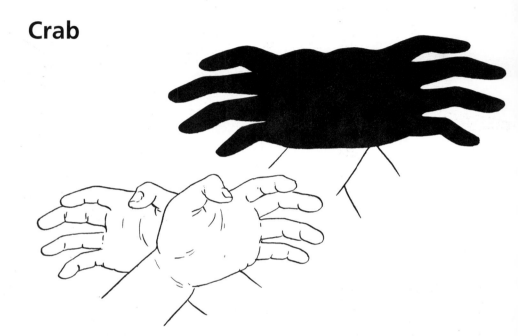

1 Hold both hands palms up.
2 Stretch out fingers.
3 Cross left hand over right hand. Wrists touching.
4 Tuck thumbs down.
5 Gently move all fingers.

Crabs move sideways.

Snail

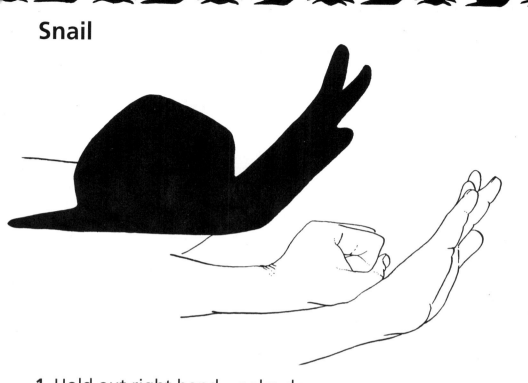

1 Hold out right hand – palm down.
2 Pull palm back so that fingers all point up.
3 Make a fist with left hand, tuck thumb inside.
4 Place fist on the back of right hand wrist.
5 Move index finger of right hand out to give the snail two horns.
6 Move thumb of right hand forwards so it lies along the front of your index finger.
7 Bend fingers gently to make the snail's horns move.

Snails move slowly.

Me and My Pet Dog

TwoCan

Be careful to keep soapy water out of your dog's eyes.

Bathtime

If you groom your dog regularly, he shouldn't need a bath. But if he rolls in something disgusting, a good scrub is the only solution! Use special dog shampoo and rinse it off well. Dry your dog with a towel and finish off with a hair dryer set to a low heat.

Don't use a hairdryer if your dog has itchy skin.

Not too hot – that's just right!

Head first

As part of the grooming routine, you should gently wash your dog's ears and nose, and bathe around his eyes with a piece of cotton wool. Then brush his teeth gently with a special toothpaste for dogs.

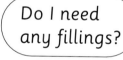

Do I need any fillings?

Keeping clean

Most dogs get very excited after they've had a bath and rush around the house at top speed. It's a good idea to keep your dog indoors for a few hours, otherwise he might roll in the mud all over again!

There is more about dogs on pages 6 and 103.

How to Cook Spaghetti

You will need 50–75 grams of dried spaghetti per person; a big saucepan of water; a large pinch of salt

Put the salt into the water and bring to the boil, then add the spaghetti. Hold the spaghetti in a bunch and put one end in the water. It will get soft and bendy. Push the spaghetti slowly down into the water until it coils round the pan. Use a fork to push the ends of the bunch into the water, and to stir the spaghetti to stop it sticking together.

Tip: add a teaspoon of cooking oil to the water, which will help to stop the pasta sticking.

Cook the pasta, uncovered, for 10–12 minutes.

Like all pasta, spaghetti should be cooked until it is still a little chewy, not sloppy.

When the spaghetti is cooked, drain it well. For a quick snack, serve with grated cheese or tomato ketchup.

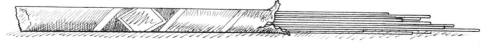

There is more about spaghetti on pages 28 and 30.

Create a Crater

GODFREY HALL

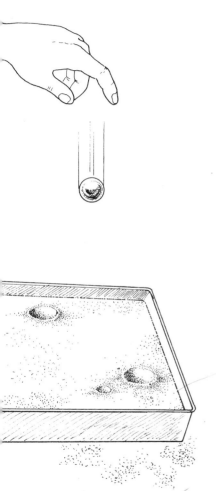

The Moon is littered with craters. Scientists believe that they were made when rocks from outer space struck the surface.

You will need:
• a large deep tin or tray • sand or flour • Plasticine • rocks • marbles • a small ball

1 Fill your tray with sand or flour.
2 Stand by the tray and drop a marble onto the surface. What happens as it hits the sand or flour?
3 Now try dropping one of the rocks and then the ball.

What happens?
Is there a difference in the size of the crater made by the marble and the ball? Try your experiment standing on a chair. Are the craters you make smaller or larger than before?

There is more about the moon and space travel on pages 31, 68, 86 and 104.

The Arctic Fox

MARY ELLIS

One evening, Alex opens the back door of her house
and sees that snow has turned the garden into
a world of strange white shapes.

Forgetting my coat, I stepped outside. The
flakes brushed against my face. My
slippers crunched in the powdery snow.
And then I saw them. *Perfectly
formed little paw prints in the snow.*
I knew they weren't Charlie's paw
prints. (He was our neighbour's
cat.) Sometimes on rainy days when
Charlie followed me into the
kitchen he left little muddy marks on
the floor. *These* prints were different.

The snow muffled my footsteps. I
followed the paw prints and they led me to our
old pine tree. Pushing back the branches, I peered
into the clearing inside. Two gleaming black eyes
gazed back at me in the darkness. I did not want to
scare it away, whatever it was. I stayed as still as I
could, hardly daring to breathe.

Quite suddenly, snow that had piled up on a nearby branch fell to the ground. It sent up a white spray. I jumped. There was a scrabbling sound from inside the tree. I just managed to catch a glimpse of a white fluffy tail as it disappeared through a hole in our fence.

I crouched down and waited, hoping that the creature with the shiny black eyes might return. Something glinted and caught my eye. I felt the snow, where it had been disturbed, under the hole in the fence. My fingers touched something hard and sharp. I looked closer. It was a *tooth*.

There is more about foxes on pages 16, 17, 79 and 93.

Vicky Fox

(FROM *WILLA AND MISS ANNIE*)
BERLIE DOHERTY

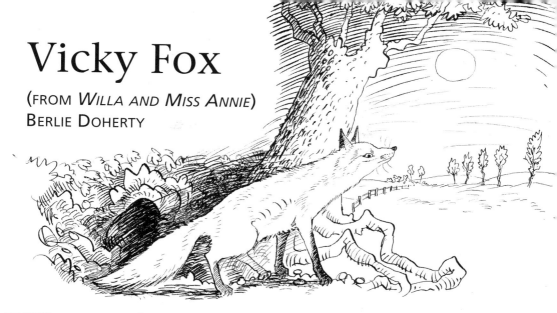

Deep in the earth it was brown and cool and it smelled of mushrooms and leaves. In the spinney woods a fox watched for the moonlight and streaked out from his lair. He put his snout to the ground to sniff out the trails he had made his own. He crossed the scents of rabbits and badgers and all the other creatures of the night. He smelled cats and dogs and human beings. He smelled the eggman's hens in the field at the edge of town.

In his lair his vixen lay with her brush-tail tucked under her chin. She watched for the fox to bring her food. Her brown cubs nuzzled each other, snug at her side, and warm with her milk.

In the houses children were sleeping. In the house at the edge of town a little girl called Ruth opened her eyes and listened. She could hear the hens screeching in the yard. She heard her father the eggman getting out of his bed, and she heard the stairs creaking. "I'll get that fox!" she heard him say. "This time I'll get him, good and proper."

Ruth heard him going out to the yard. She could hear him untying the dogs.

"You shouldn't, you shouldn't," the little girl cried. "Killing the lovely foxes is cruel."

And that was the night that the fox died. The dogs ran out to meet him, and he never went home again. The dogs ran on to the vixen's lair and found the vixen with her brush tucked under her chin. They found the nuzzling cubs that were warm with her milk by her side. And when the eggman whistled them home they left them all for dead.

But one of the cubs was still alive. She whimpered for her mother to give her milk. She whimpered for her brothers and sisters to nuzzle her. She whimpered for her father to come home.

But nobody answered her.

The moon went dark, and all night long it rained. The rain hissed like long snakes, and all the leaves pattered and gleamed.

The fox cub curled up with the brush under her chin and waited for food.

There is more about foxes on pages 16, 17, 76 and 93.

Beetle and the Biosphere

SUSAN GATES

> Abby has been collecting ladybirds. Now she's on her
> way back to her Grandma's thinking about food.

"I'll have peanut butter sandwiches," decided
Abby, as she started back to Grandma's house.

No one could call the dunes beautiful. Here
and there was a hollow of fine white sand
sprinkled with pink and yellow snail shells. But
mostly the hills were scrubby with sea
buckthorn and hawthorn. Razor-sharp grasses
sliced your ankles. Rabbits left droppings
everywhere in neat little piles that grew white
and crumbly with age.

"Or maybe a sugar and banana sandwich."

Abby was walking through a green corridor.
There were masses of these narrow tracks,
crisscrossing the dunes, tunnelling through the
spikiest vegetation. Abby knew them like the
back of her hand. She spent most school

holidays down here with Grandma Spooner.

"And a Coke."

A hand was resting in the middle of the mossy path.

Its fingers were white, curled up like a huge dead spider.

"Urgh!" Abby's whole body jerked in horror. She backed away from the clutching hand. And dropped her box of ladybirds.

There was an old man sprawled among the buckthorn bushes. The branches were splintered as if he had crash-landed there.

Queasy, with her stomach clenched up like a sea anemone, Abby tiptoed closer.

"It's a dead body," she whispered, appalled.

He looked dead. He looked as if he'd been here for ages. As if he were part of the dunes. His white hair sparkled. It sparkled because busy spiders had already colonized it and the morning dew was glittering in their webs.

Cautiously, on wobbly legs, Abby plucked a thorny branch aside so she could see his face.

"Mr Robinson!"

It was her grandma's neighbour – the only person, apart from Grandma, who lived all year in the summer houses.

His eyes blinked open.

Abby's terror collapsed. Urgency took over.

"Mr Robinson! Mr Robinson!"

She knelt down on crunchy snail shells. She touched his face, to make him look at her. His skin was cold and clammy, like sand before the sun warms it. A big white moth, hidden in his hair, flopped into Abby's hand. He must have been lying here all night. Abby shook the moth into the grass.

"It's Abby, Mr Robinson. Abby from next door. What happened? What are you doing out here? ◼

The Eagle has Landed

(FROM *SPACE STORIES THAT REALLY HAPPENED*)
ANDREW DONKIN

On the 21st of July 1969 Neil Armstrong climbed out of a spacecraft called *Apollo 11* and became the first human being to stand on the surface of the moon.

He got ready to step off the ladder.

Neil Armstrong knew that the first words spoken on the moon would go down in history. He had not known what he was going to say until just a few minutes ago, but now he was certain.

"That's one small step for man," he said as his boot touched the surface, "one giant leap for mankind."

He let go of the ship's ladder and walked away from the Lunar Modular with a strange slow-motion bounce.

Mankind was on the moon.

A few moments later, Buzz Aldrin joined him on the surface. He gazed round at the rocks and craters that stretched as far as the eye could see.

"Beautiful."

"Isn't it something?" agreed Armstrong.

After all their training and planning, nothing had prepared them for the actual moon itself.

As they looked around they saw that they had touched down on a wide plain. There were rocks and sharp boulders lying around and a number of craters dented the surface.

Beneath their moon boots, the surface seemed to be covered in a layer of dust a few centimetres thick, with a rocky surface underneath it.

The sky above them was black, with the Earth shining like a blue jewel.

There is more about the moon and space travel on pages 31, 68, 75 and 104.

The Owl Tree

JENNY NIMMO

> Joe doesn't know why, but he's just got to get out of
> bed and climb the huge and mysterious tree that
> grows in Mr Rock's garden. Joe loves this beautiful
> tree. But Mr Rock wants to cut it down…

The owl-tree shone pearl-grey in the night, its golden leaves turned to silver. Joe found a foot-hold and began to climb. The tree slipped branches under his feet and swept them close to his hands. Joe pulled himself up to the sky.

Higher and higher. Now the houses were far below and he could see chinks of light from bedroom windows.

"I'm here," Joe told the tree. "So tell me how to save you." The tree whispered and sighed, "Higher... Higher..." How high would he have to go before he had an answer? He put his ear against the trunk and heard a heartbeat deep inside.

"Tell me," Joe begged.

There was a movement above him, the beginning of an answer. And then it came – a shriek and a wild, white thrashing over his head. And Joe, too frightened to cry out, was falling, falling, falling! ■

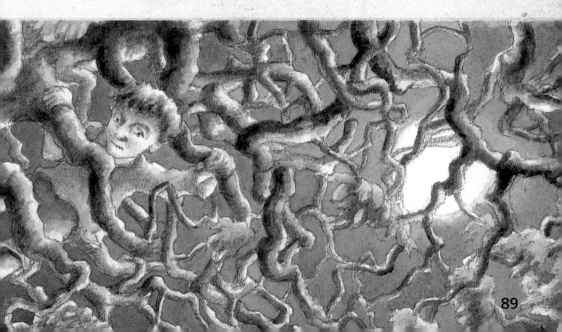

The Stone Mouse

JENNY NIMMO

The stone mouse is very special to Elly, and this makes her brother Ted angry. Ted is sad and angry about lots of things at the moment. "That mouse is just a dirty old pebble," he says. But is that what he really thinks?

Ted had reached the bottom of the steps. He took the stone mouse out of his pocket but he didn't look at it. He didn't want to see the glint of a tiny eye or the stirring of a whisker. The shore sparkled with wet pebbles. Ted approached the waves.

"Don't," pleaded the stone mouse, reading the danger signals. "It won't make you feel any better."

"It will," Ted shouted in sudden fury. He raised his arm and flung the stone mouse at the clouds.

"Elly!" called the mouse as he spun into the sky. "Help me!" But his voice was lost in the wind and drowned by the tumbling sea.

"Elly!" the mouse sighed in despair. He hit the ocean with a splash that stunned him, and dropped through the cold gloomy water without any sense of where or what he was. Though, just before he sank onto a bed of seaweed, he managed to whisper, "I'm just a stone after all."

And yet he wasn't just a stone!

A moon appeared above the water and fingers of light crept about the ocean floor, showing the mouse that he hadn't lost his mousy curiosity.

The gleaming shapes that crawled and darted all about him were talkative and friendly. Only the pebbles worried him, with their smooth, eyeless surfaces and lack of conversation. They made him sad and even more determined to be an animal.

The Red Secret

JENNY NIMMO

Tom is trying to look after an injured foxcub. He has hidden it in the garden shed, but dogs have found it and tried to attack it. Now Tom has to get the cub to a safer and more secret place.

Tom could feel his heart thumping as he ran through the wood. He was a little scared of what he was doing: running alone through a silent wood, long before breakfast, with Mum not knowing where he was. But one thing he was sure of; he had to save Rufus and he had to keep him secret.

He came to the stone house sooner than he expected. He must have run very fast. Tom wrenched open the door. It was extraordinary, and so lucky, that the thick oak door had remained, while the roof had all but rotted away. The little cub would have a carpet of moss and cobbles, sky and branches above his head, and four high stone walls to keep him safe.

Tom went into the small room at the end of the stone house, where the roof still remained. A few tiles were missing but it was dark and dry in the corner where the table stood. Tom knelt down and gently removed the bundle from his bag. The foxcub rolled out of Mr Turner's jacket and lay glaring at Tom.

"I know you're frightened and your leg hurts," Tom said. "But I wish you could like me. I'm trying to help." He took out the plastic box, opened it and placed it beside the cub.

Still glaring, and making a strange, angry noise, the cub edged closer to the cold shepherd's pie. He was confused and terrified after his undignified journey, but he was hungry too. He began to eat.

There is more about foxes on pages 16, 17, 76 and 79.

The Octopus

OGDEN NASH

Tell me, O Octopus, I begs,
Is those things arms, or is they legs?
I marvel at thee, Octopus;
If I were thou, I'd call me Us.

Twickham Tweer

JACK PRELUTSKY

Shed a tear for Twickham Tweer
who ate uncommon meals,
who often peeled bananas
and then only ate the peels,
who emptied jars of marmalade
and only ate the jars,
and only ate the wrappers
off of chocolate candy bars.

When Twickham cooked a chicken
he would only eat the bones,
he discarded scoops of ice cream
though he always ate the cones,
he'd boil a small potato
but he'd only eat the skin,
and pass up canned asparagus
to gobble down the tin.

He sometimes dined on apple cores
and bags of peanut shells,
on cottage cheese containers,
cellophane from caramels,
but Twickham Tweer passed on last year,
that odd and novel man,
when he fried an egg one morning
and then ate the frying pan.

It's Dark in Here

SHEL SILVERSTEIN

I am writing these poems
From inside a lion,
And it's rather dark in here.
So please excuse the handwriting
Which may not be too clear.
But this afternoon by the lion's cage
I'm afraid I got too near.
And I'm writing these lines
From inside a lion,
And it's rather dark in here.

Eletelephony

LAURA E. RICHARDS

Once there was an elephant,
Who tried to use the telephant –
No! No! I mean an elephone
Who tried to use the telephone –
(Dear me! I am not certain quite
That even now I've got it right.)

Howe'er it was, he got his trunk
Entangled in the telephunk;
The more he tried to get it free,
The louder buzzed the telephee –
(I fear I'd better drop the song
Of elephop and telephong!)

Windy Nights

RODNEY BENNETT

Rumbling in the chimneys,
Rattling at the doors,
Round the roofs and round the roads
The rude wind roars;
Raging through the darkness,
Raving through the trees,
Racing off again across
The great grey seas.

Weather

EVE MERRIAM

Dot a dot dot dot a dot dot
Spotting the windowpane.

Spack a spack speck flick a flack fleck
Freckling the windowpane.

A spatter a scatter a wet cat a clatter
A splatter a rumble outside.

Umbrella umbrella umbrella umbrella
Bumbershoot barrel of rain.

Slosh a galosh slosh a galosh
Slither and slather a glide

A puddle a jump a puddle a jump
A puddle a jump puddle splosh

A juddle a pump a luddle a dump
A pudmuddle jump in and slide!

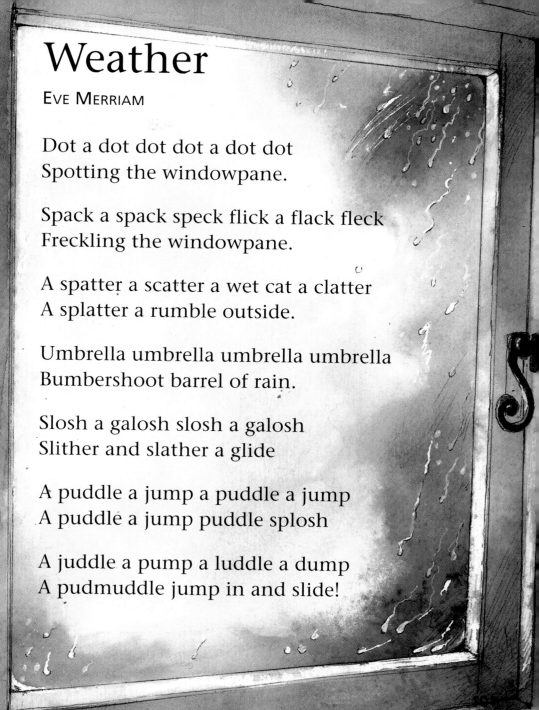

Kingfisher Children's Encyclopedia

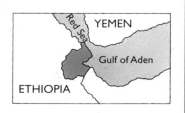

Government: Republic
Capital: Djibouti
Area: 22,000 sq km
Population: 327,000
Language: French
Currency: Djibouti franc

Diving *see* Underwater Exploration

Djibouti

The small republic of Djibouti is in north-east Africa beside the Red Sea. It is about the size of Wales and has a population of 327,000. Much of the country is desert and there are few natural resources. About a third of the people are nomads who rear goats, cattle and camels. The country's capital is also called Djibouti, a port that handles most of the exports from neighbouring ETHIOPIA. Djibouti gained independence from France in 1977.

Dodo

About 400 years ago a Dutch ship landed explorers on Mauritius, a lonely island in the Indian Ocean. They found doves, fish and large flocks of birds as big and fat as turkeys. These birds had no proper wings and could not fly. In time people called them dodos, from the Portuguese word *doudo*. This word means 'simpleton' or a stupid person. Sailors quickly learnt that dodos were

The dodo was said to have a cry like a gosling. It laid one white egg on a nest of grass.

good to eat. Ships that visited Mauritius sailed off with holds full of salted dodo meat. Rats and dogs from the ships started eating dodo eggs and chicks.

By the 1690s all the dodos were dead. Only drawings, bones and one stuffed bird remained.

Dog

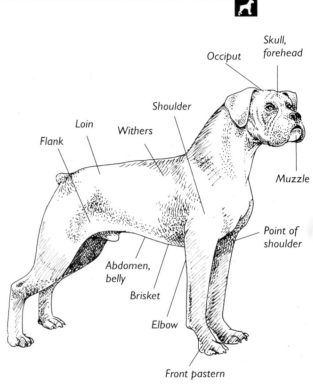

People have been keeping dogs for perhaps 10,000 years. Most dogs are kept as pets but some do useful work like herding sheep or guarding buildings.

The first dog was probably descended from a WOLF and looked much like a wolf. Today there are more than 100 breeds of dog of many colours, shapes, and sizes. The St Bernard is the largest breed. A St Bernard may weigh nearly twice as much as a man. The Yorkshire terrier is one of the smallest dogs. A fully grown Yorkshire terrier may weigh less than a small pot of jam.

Skull, forehead

Occiput

Shoulder

Loin

Withers

Flank

Muzzle

Point of shoulder

Abdomen, belly

Brisket

Elbow

Front pastern

The main parts of a dog are shown on this picture of a Boxer.

 There is more about dogs on pages 6 and 72.

Moon

The next-door neighbour of Earth in space is the Moon – a ball of rock that spins on its own axis as well as orbiting the Earth and travelling with the Earth as it orbits the Sun. It is one of the best studied objects in the Solar System. Detailed maps of the side that faces Earth were drawn soon after the invention of the telescope. In the 1960s, space probes were sent crashing into its surface, and orbiting around it. In 1969, people even walked on the Moon, and brought back rocks from its surface. All the Solar System planets except Mercury and Venus have moons. They range a great deal in size, but Earth's moon is one of the largest – around one quarter of the size of Earth.

LUNAR LANDINGS

The seventeen Apollo missions of the 1960s and 1970s are still regarded as the high point of space exploration. These missions set twelve astronauts on the Moon and returned them safely back to Earth.

MOON WATCHING

The moon is a good object for novice astronomers to observe because its surface features are easily visible to the naked eye. The dark patches that can be seen are flat areas of land called "maria". The lighter areas are mountains. Binoculars can even reveal some of the craters that cover much of the Moon's surface.

MOON ROCK

Around 2,000 samples of moon rock, weighing almost 400 kg (880 lb), have been brought back to Earth. By studying these rocks, scientists have built up a picture of the composition and history of the Moon. Some rocks, for example, were formed from molten lava.

There is more about the moon and space travel on pages 31, 68, 75 and 86.

The Ladybird Question

Mr Steven Greening
C/o Oxford University Press
Oxford

Joe Stevenson
Class 3LR
Mill Park Community School
Lowdon
West Yorkshire

19 January 2000

Dear Mr Greening,

I read your book called The Secret Life of Insects. It was really good. The best bit was about the praying mantis with the big picture in it. I really like insects and I think they are interesting. My best friend called Leon doesn't like them. He says that the picture of the spider's face made him feel sick.

Please will you answer a question for me? I asked Mrs Rowe but she did not know. She said why don't I write to you and ask, so I am.

My question is where do ladybirds go in the winter? Do they go to sleep or do they die and then new ones are born in the spring?

I hope you are not too busy to answer.

Yours sincerely,

Joe Stevenson
(Aged 8)

The Ladybird Reply

Steven Greening
C/o O.U.P.
Oxford

Jan. 25th

Dear Joe,

Thanks for your letter. I'm glad you enjoyed my book. Your question is a very good one. The answer is that ladybirds do hibernate (sleep through the winter). And they hibernate in huge groups. Sometimes hundreds or even thousands of ladybirds all sleep together in the same place.

So how come we never see these masses of sleeping ladybirds? They are very good at finding hiding places, like a space deep inside an old stone wall or under the bark of a tree. The only way of knowing where they are is to see them all going in there at the beginning of winter. You'd have to be very lucky to notice that.

I'm glad you wrote, because I think I was a bit silly not to put this information in the book. If I write another book about insect secrets I'll make sure I put it in.

Thanks again for writing,

Best wishes,

Letters from Antarctica

SARA WHEELER

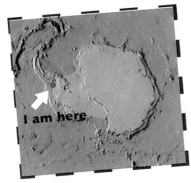

I am here

Fossil Bluff
Sunday 8 January

Dear Daniel
I have never seen so
much ice, and so many different kinds of it
too. Antarctica has 90 per cent of the whole
world's ice, and in some places it is 1,500
metres deep. Around the edge of the
continent even the sea is frozen sometimes,
and I often pitch my own tent on it. You
have to drill a long way to get through this
lid of ice over the sea, but when you do,
there are fish living in the chilly waters
underneath. They have special anti-freeze in
their blood to stop them from icing up.

I am sending you photographs of some of the different kinds of ice I have seen.

Love,

Sara

Ice crystal flowers forming on frozen sea.

A fantastic natural ice sculpture on Mount Erebus.

An iceberg trapped in frozen sea.

A noticeboard

Party!

Dear . Ravi . . . .
Please come to . Zoe's . . . . . party
On .Friday. 6th July. . . . .
At .18. Bicton Road . . . .
From 5.30 p.m. until . 7.30.p.m. .

Tomatoes
onions
garlic
spaghetti
cheese
b.day card
kite?
wrapping paper

Budmouth Community Primary School

Parents' Evening

Dear Mr. and Mrs. Chatterji...........

We have made an appointment for you and
.Ravi.......... to talk to .Mr. Stevenson.... at
...6.20. pm...... on Thursday. July. 5th.

We hope you will be able to attend.

10 METRES